GRAMMAR
PUNCTUATION & SPELLING

SATs
CHALLENGE
YEAR 6

Skills Tests

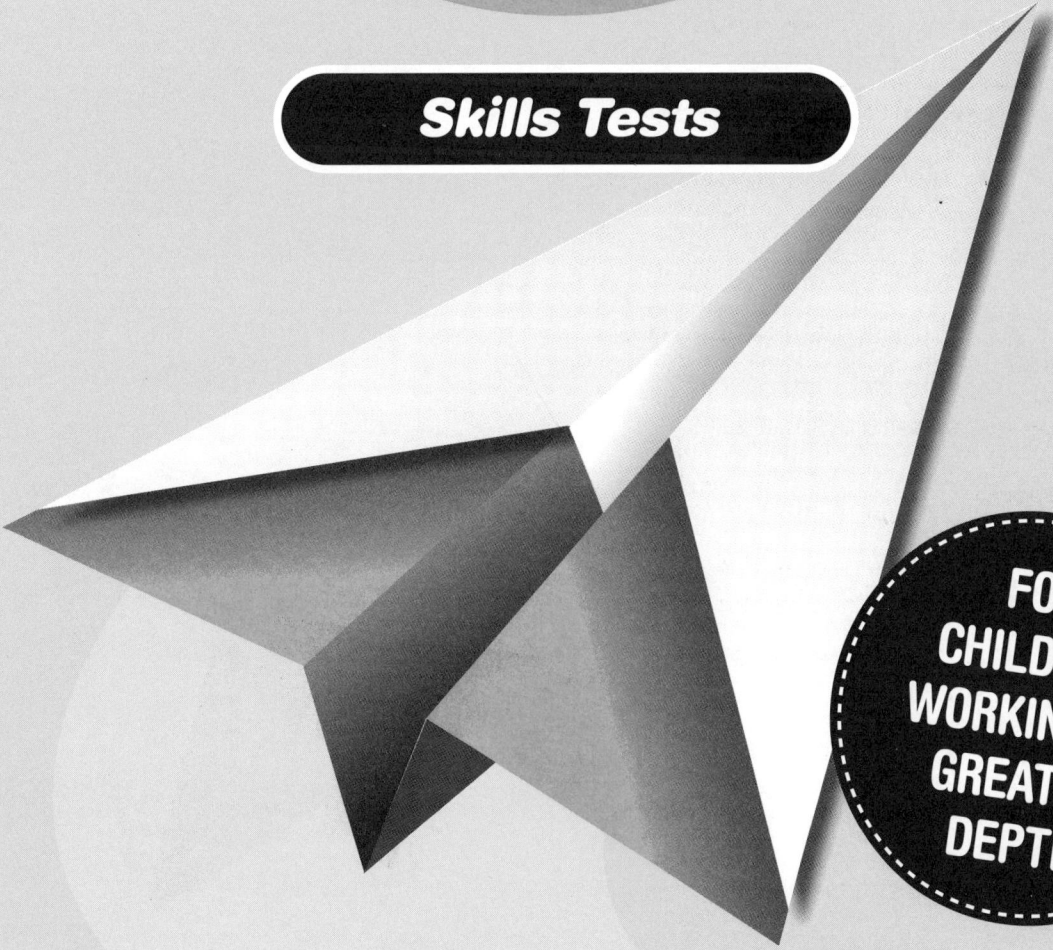

FOR CHILDREN WORKING AT GREATER DEPTH

Book End, Range Road, Witney, Oxfordshire, OX29 0YD
Registered office: Westfield Road, Southam, Warwickshire CV47 0RA
www.scholastic.co.uk

© 2020, Scholastic Ltd

1 2 3 4 5 6 7 8 9   8 9 0 1 2 3 4 5 6 7

British Library Cataloguing-in-Publication Data
A catalogue record for this book is available from the British Library.

ISBN 978-1407-18369-5
Printed and bound by Replika Press, India

Author
Shelley Welsh

Editorial
Rachel Morgan, Shannon Keenlyside, Audrey Stokes, Louise Titley,
Margaret Eaton, Julia Roberts

Series Design
Scholastic Design Team: Nicolle Thomas and Neil Salt

Layout
Couper Street Type Co

Cover Design
Scholastic Design Team: Nicolle Thomas and Neil Salt

Contents

Advice for parents and carers

Children learn best when they do not feel under pressure and when they are free to explore ideas. Be flexible. If your child is distracted or tired they will not gain much from the practice.

This book allows children to apply what they have learned in key areas of the curriculum. The questions have been written to a higher level than usual and are meant to be challenging and to provide stretch. Supporting learning and understanding in this way will strengthen your child's grasp of key concepts. The questions can be used to assess areas to work on further. Follow up by offering opportunities to consolidate learning in a real-life setting and allow a break before working on further questions.

Please note that if your child does not do well in answering these questions it is not an indication of poor performance in the National Tests. If you have any concerns, please discuss them with your child's teacher.

Use these tests however works best for you and your child but you may want to follow this approach:

- Ask your child to complete Section 1. There is no need to time this test or complete it in one sitting.

- Mark the test using the answers on pages 73–76.

- Use the answer grids on pages 84–85 to identify which areas your child needs more practice.

- Review these areas and practice skills in the related *Workbook (ISBN 978-1407-17651-2)*. Use the links in the answer grids to direct you to units you may wish to focus on or work through the *Workbook* unit by unit.

- Once you feel your child has had enough opportunity to build up their skills, complete Section 3 and mark it to assess their progress. Review topics as necessary.

There are two spelling tests included in this book which are in the same format as the test your child will be taking. Use the guidance on pages 71 and 72 to help you administer these tests.

Advice for children

Are you ready to take the challenge? The questions in this book are tricky but they will help you to see how much you understand.

Don't worry if you don't manage to answer every question or if you get some answers wrong. We learn from our mistakes.

- Find a quiet place to work.

- Have a positive mindset – focus on what you know. Remember that mistakes make our brain grows!

- Take your time – don't start the challenge if you are in a rush to do something else.

- Review your work.

Progress chart

Section	Test	Taken	Practised	Achieved
1	All topic areas			
	Spelling			
2	Word classes			
	Functions of sentences			
	Combining words, phrases and clauses			
	Verb forms, tense and consistency			
	Punctuation			
	Vocabulary			
	Standard English and formality			
3	All topic areas			
	Spelling			

Reward Certificate

Well done!

I've aimed higher with SATs Challenge

Name: _Chrissa_   Date: _____

My strongest areas are:

_____

_____

I will challenge myself to fly higher in:

_____

SECTION 1: ALL TOPIC AREAS

Marks

1. Underline the **adjectives** in this sentence.

As the galloping horses cleared the final fence,

the crowd applauded wildly.

1

2. Complete the following sentences using the **past progressive form** of the verbs in brackets.

a. Just as we ___approached___ (approach) our destination, the traffic became more and more congested.

1

b. My sister Megan ___arranged___ (arrange) flowers in a vase for Mum.

1

3. Insert the missing **apostrophes** in the correct places in the passage below.

Its been five years since Ive seen my cousin's, Stephane and Anya. Stephane's dress-sense was always slightly unusual and Anya's smile was infectious. Mum's very excited about seeing her sister again and shes promised well all go out for a meal as soon as they've unpacked.

2

Marks

4. What is the **function** of the sentence below?

Don't cross the road without looking left and right first

Tick **one**.

Statement ☐

Command ☑

Exclamation ☐

Question ☐

1

5. Write a suitable **relative clause** to complete the sentence below.

Our teacher Mr Harrison, who was ~~wean~~ working in the school for over 30 years, is retiring next year.

1

6. Underline the **subject** and circle the **object** in the sentences below.

a. Ciara's mum was pleased with her presents.

b. Some careless person has left the door open.

1

7. Add a **prefix** to each word below to make its **antonym**.

_____practical

_____decided

_____accessible

_____legitimate

Marks

1

8. Complete the sentence below with a suitable verb in the **present perfect tense**.

We _____ in the same house for ten years.

1

9. Use appropriate **punctuation** to complete the sentence below.

At the circus, we saw the following trapeze artists performing ponies a high-wire act and a rather sad clown

1

10. Write a **question** that could generate the answer below.

Question: _How was the weather in France, tomorrow?_

Answer: Supposedly hot and sunny but there might be showers in the evening.

1

Marks

11.   Add a suitable **fronted adverbial** to complete this sentence.

_____ we eventually reached the summit.

1

12.   How does adding the **prefix** <u>mis</u> to the words below change their meaning?

| shaped | understand | spell | judge |

Tick **one**.

They become nouns. ☐

They become verbs. ☐

They mean the opposite. ☐

The tense changes. ☐

1

13.   Complete the sentence below so that the verb form uses the **subjunctive mood**.

If I _____ to approach the manager in the correct way, I am positive he would respond favourably to my request.

1

14. Underline the **adverbs** in the sentence below.

After we had eaten our breakfast, we quickly tidied up and went outside.

Marks

1

15. Insert **commas** to indicate **parenthesis** in the sentence below.

Our former neighbours John and Josephine came to visit us today.

1

16. Insert a **relative pronoun** in each sentence below.

a. The little boy, _____ parents were late to pick him up, was very upset.

1

b. Our grandparents, with _____ we stay every summer, are coming to visit us this year.

1

17. Complete the sentence below by adding a suitable **conjunction**.

Dad likes to listen to music on his headphones _____ he cuts the grass.

1

18. Tick one box in each row to indicate the **word class** of each word in this sentence.

Our old dog always shivers when he is cold.

Sentence	Adjective	Adverb	Verb	Pronoun	Possessive determiner	Noun	Conjunction
Our							
old							
dog							
always							
shivers							
when							
he							
is							
cold							

Marks

1

19. Add a **suffix** to change each adjective into a noun. Remember to make any necessary changes to spelling.

pretty → _____

empty → _____

full → _____

1

20. Add a **modal verb** to indicate possibility in the sentence below.

We _____ go to Spain for our holidays this year.

1

Marks

21. Underline the **possessive pronouns** in the sentences below.

Those cakes are mine; I made them in school today.

Khalid made some too but his are slightly burnt.

1

22. Insert the missing **punctuation** in the **direct speech** below.

We need to pack our clothes tonight said Mum

Can't I wait until the morning I asked

It will be too rushed if you leave it until the morning

she replied

1

23. Add a **prefix** to each word below to make its **antonym**.

_____regular

_____continue

_____reliable

_____probable

1

24. Underline all the **determiners** in the sentence below.

Some people eat their lunch on the field on sunny days,

but I prefer to stay in the shade.

1

Marks

25. Millie said, "Commas are only for separating items in a list."

Is Millie correct? Circle either **Yes** or **No**.

Yes   No

Explain your reason.

_____

_____

1

26. Tick the sentence that uses a **dash** correctly.

Tick **one**.

Liam crept cautiously towards the entrance – to the cave surely the creature was no longer there? ☐

Liam crept cautiously towards the entrance to the cave surely – the creature was no longer there? ☐

Liam crept cautiously towards the entrance to the cave – surely the creature was no longer there? ☐

Liam – crept cautiously towards the entrance to the cave surely the creature was no longer there? ☐

1

Marks

27. Tick one box in each row to indicate whether the word <u>after</u> is used as a **subordinating conjunction** or as a **preposition**.

Sentence	<u>after</u> used as a subordinating conjunction	<u>after</u> used as a preposition
<u>After</u> I had finished my homework, I watched a film with Dad.		
The animals in the zoo like to snooze <u>after</u> they've eaten.		
I'm going to Ushma's house <u>after</u> school.		

1

28. Which sentence below functions as a **statement**?

Tick **one**.

Come to my house to watch the tennis later ☐

The aerial on our roof needs to be fixed ☐

There are only three more weeks of school left, aren't there ☐

Please don't forget to text me the homework later ☐

1

29. Rewrite the **active voice** sentence below in the **passive voice**.

While we were away, our neighbour looked after our pet tortoise.

_____

_____

1

Marks

30. Which sentence below functions as an **exclamation**?

Tick **one**.

We were relieved to be boarding the plane at long last ☐

How excited I was ☐

If I were magic, I could teleport myself across the Atlantic ☐

Sadly, we will just have to be patient ☐

1

31. Rewrite the sentence below so that it starts with the **adverbial**.

Luke and Heba were exhausted after their long hike up the mountain.

_____

_____

1

32. Use only the words in the boxes below to make a sentence.

| who has just moved house | my friend Bethan |

| is coming to stay | this weekend |

_____

_____

_____

1

Marks

33. Underline the **expanded noun phrase** in the sentence below.

After a long, hard day, Jo was glad to get home and relax on the settee.

1

34. Tick the sentence below that uses **Standard English**.

Tick **one**.

Pick up them books for me, please. ☐

There's no point in worrying about the test. ☐

We seen that film already. ☐

There is twenty girls and ten boys in my class. ☐

1

35. Rewrite the sentence below in the **present perfect tense**.

I ate some interesting dishes during my holiday.

_____

_____

1

36. Choose the **suffix ify**, **ise** or **ate** to make each word below a verb. Write the verb on the line next to each.

priority _____

sign _____

indication _____

1

37. Complete the sentences below using either **I** or **me**.

Our teacher handed Freya and _____ our books.

Freya and _____ were thrilled with our results.

1

38. Write the **plural forms** of the words below.

church _____

child _____

piano _____

class _____

1

39. Insert the final **punctuation marks** in each of the following sentences.

What a wonderful day that was

Do you think we can do it again soon

The weather forecast looks promising for tomorrow

What time do you think we should meet

1

40. Insert **commas for clarity** in the following sentence.

We have decided since the snow seems to be sticking that we will go sledging in the park.

1

Marks

41. Underline the word that does not belong in the **word family** below.

signal   signature   sigh   sign   signet

1

42. Underline the **possessive determiners** in the sentence below.

Their grandparents are thinking of moving closer

to our neighbourhood so that they can see more of

their grandchildren.

1

43. Tick the sentence where there is **tense consistency**.

Tick **one**.

We walk to the park but we took the bus home. ☐

It has been a long day but thankfully we were home now. ☐

I have been waiting for a new bike for ages and now my wait had been over. ☐

We had finished our jobs so we were free to play. ☐

1

44. Place a tick in each row to say whether each genre is **formal** or **informal**.

Genre	Formal	Informal
Diary writing		
Presentation in a job interview		
Postcard		
Persuasive letter to the local council		

1

Marks

45. Write the **contracted form** for each group of words below.

have not _____

you will _____

she has _____

shall not _____

1

46. Rewrite the sentence below in the **present progressive tense**.

Mel jumps on the trampoline.

_____

1

47. Complete the sentence below with a suitable **relative pronoun**.

There are the boys _____ bikes were stolen yesterday.

1

48. Rewrite the sentence below replacing the proper nouns in bold with a **pronoun**.

Bethan and Freddy are good friends; **Bethan and Freddy** have known each other for years.

_____

_____

1

Marks

49. Rewrite the sentence below, expanding the **noun phrases** in bold.

The butterfly fluttered over **the flowers** and landed on **a bush**.

_____

_____

_____

1

50. Complete the sentence below with a **modal verb** to indicate certainty.

Next week, Leila _____ take her Grade 3 piano exam.

1

51. Write a **synonym** to replace the word in bold.

The pyramid was **unbelievably** tall.

_____

1

52. Complete the sentence below so that it is in the **past perfect tense**.

After we _____ to the zoo, we went for something to eat.

1

Marks

53. Rewrite the **passive voice** sentences below in the **active voice.**

Passive voice	Active voice
Our car was washed by an expert cleaning crew.	
After I twisted my ankle, I was helped up the stairs by my friend Anna.	

1

54. Why have **commas** been used in the sentence below?

My uncle, the one who lives in Australia, is coming to stay at Christmas.

Tick **one**.

To separate items in a list. ☐

To indicate possession. ☐

To indicate parenthesis. ☐

To indicate a relative clause. ☐

1

Marks

55. Rewrite the sentence below so that it starts with the **subordinate clause**.

The runners began to fantasise about a cold drink and a hot bath as they neared the end of the marathon.

_____

_____

_____

1

56. Show two ways the missing **apostrophe** could be inserted in each sentence below. Explain why you have chosen each position.

1. The naughty girl picked off the flowers petals one by one.

Explanation: _____

_____

_____

1

2. The naughty girl picked off the flowers petals one by one.

Explanation: _____

_____

_____

1

Marks

57. Underline the **subject** and circle the **object** in the sentence below.

1

The bird suddenly swooped down towards its nest.

58. Add a suitable **prefix** to each word below.

_____matic

_____human

_____fortune

1

_____view

59. Underline the **adverb** in the sentence below.

Sam worked hard on her school project but it was

1

worth it.

60. Underline three **nouns** in the sentence below.

The girl showed a lot of courage when faced with

1

the ugly creature.

61. Write the tense of the **verbs in bold** in the box above each.

Marks

| simple past | past perfect | past progressive |

We **were walking** towards the park when we **saw** a fire engine

flying down the road. We **had seen** an ambulance go past only

ten minutes before. Hopefully, no one **had been** badly hurt.

1

62. Rewrite the sentence below so that the **object** becomes the **subject**.

The cat chased the mouse around the garden.

_____

_____

1

End of test

Marks

SECTION 1: SPELLING

See Spelling 1 guidance on page 69.
Each correct spelling is worth one mark.

1. My brother can be very _____

    in the mornings.

2. The villagers were very annoyed about the

    _____ of the church hall.

3. Sinead _____ her mum a bunch

    of flowers.

4. The pilot was given _____ to land.

5. We have two _____ lessons per week.

6. Stella displayed great _____ as she

    prepared to dive.

7. My mum uses a sewing _____ to make

    curtains.

8. We took games to _____ ourselves on the

    long flight.

9. The scar on my finger is now hardly _____.

10. Dad's new boss is _____, extrovert and

    fun-loving.

10

Marks

11. Juan _____ goes to Spain in the holidays.

12. Mum gave Dad _____ instructions about preparing the meal.

13. Summer term is _____ the best.

14. My _____ best friend believes everything I tell him!

15. Billy and I _____ the last piece of cake.

16. The children were _____ to get to the seaside.

17. The _____ made a speech about his party's policy.

18. The Queen has had the longest _____ of any British monarch.

19. I staggered under the _____ of the heavy box.

20. Our teacher _____ us for talking in assembly.

10

End of test

SECTION 2: WORD CLASSES

1. **a.** Write a sentence using the word <u>hike</u> as a **noun**.

    _____

    1

    b. Write a sentence using the word <u>hike</u> as a **verb**.

    _____

    1

2. Write the correct label in each box to show the **word class**.

verb A	noun B	adjective C	adverb D

    Finally, we reached the island which was surrounded by crashing waves.

    ⬆   ⬆   ⬆   ⬆

    ☐   ☐   ☐   ☐

    1

3. Underline the **pronouns** in the sentence below.

    We gave Mia a present and she was pleased with it.

    1

4. Complete the sentence with an **adjective** formed from the verb <u>understand</u>.

    Our teacher was very _____ when we handed our homework in late.

    1

Marks

5. Complete the table below by adding a **suffix** to each **noun** to make an **adjective**.

Noun	Adjective
care	
noise	
pity	
beauty	

1

6. Insert suitable **demonstrative determiners** in the sentence below.

_____ dogs are barking at _____ postman.

1

7. Insert suitable **possessive determiners** in the sentence below.

Archie passed the butter to _____ sister so she could

butter _____ toast.

1

8. Is the word <u>fast</u> used as an **adverb** or an **adjective** in the sentence below?

We took a fast train to London and got there with time to spare.

_____

Explain how you know.

_____

1

End of test

Marks

SECTION 2: FUNCTIONS OF SENTENCES

1. Which of the following sentences is a **statement**?

Tick **one**.

Write your name at the top of the page ☐

It's quite cold today, isn't it ☐

My mum makes a great Sunday roast dinner ☐

What big teeth you've got, Grandma ☐

1

2. Rearrange the words in the question below to make it a **statement**. Remember to punctuate your sentence correctly. Do not use any additional words.

Is that girl from our town?

_____

1

3. Write a **question** that would generate the following answer.

Question	Answer
	One dog and two cats.

1

2: Functions of sentences

4. Complete the sentence below with a suitable **imperative verb**.

Please _____ your homework before the weekend.

1

5. Add a tag to this sentence to make it a **question**.

The bus is late today _____

1

6. Draw lines to match each sentence below to its function.

How many days until Christmas	statement
How excited I am about Christmas	question
There are thirteen days until Christmas	command
Tell me how many days there are until Christmas	exclamation

End of test

1

Marks

SECTION 2: COMBINING WORDS, PHRASES AND CLAUSES

1. Tick one box in each row to indicate whether each sentence contains a **subordinating conjunction** or a **co-ordinating conjunction**.

Sentence	Subordinating conjunction	Co-ordinating conjunction
We have been playing rounders and tennis this term.		
Before I leave for school, I always make my packed lunch.		
It's been quite cold, yet it's not quite the end of summer.		
I saw your cousin in the library, but I couldn't remember her name.		

1

2. Insert a suitable **subordinating conjunction** in the sentence below.

Our teacher said we would stay in at break _____ we behaved.

1

Marks

3. What is the name of the underlined **clause** in the sentence below?

Our doctor, <u>who has treated our family for years</u>, is retiring in the autumn.

_____

1

4. Underline the **expanded noun phrase** in the sentence below.

With only minutes to go, the exhausted runners pushed themselves towards the finish.

1

5. What is the **type of clause** in bold in the sentence below?

The main attraction – in my opinion, anyway – **is the fire-eating gymnast.**

_____

1

6. Insert a suitable **relative clause** in the sentence below.

My new school, _____

_____ , has lots of extra-curricular activities.

1

End of test

Marks

SECTION 2: VERB FORMS, TENSE AND CONSISTENCY

1. Tick the sentence that uses the **past progressive tense**.

Tick **one**.

We were thinking of going to the cinema but now we've changed our minds. ☐

Mum had been planning to go away with her sister until she was offered a promotion at work. ☐

There was a big roar as the home team scored the winning goal. ☐

After my dog has eaten his food, he always lies down for a snooze. ☐

1

2. Tick the sentence that is written in the **passive voice**.

Tick **one**.

We boarded the plane and took our seats by the window. ☐

I was given a choice of salad or vegetables. ☐

Izumu won the singing competition in the end-of-year show. ☐

We walk to school on the footpath that takes us over the bridge. ☐

1

3. Tick the correct box to show the **tense** of each verb on the left.

Marks

Verb	Simple present	Simple past	Present progressive	Past progressive	Present perfect	Past perfect
they were thinking						
we have seen						
Pippa plays						
you had written						
George is eating						
she spoke						

1

4. Rewrite these sentences, changing the underlined verbs to the **past progressive tense**.

a. We <u>hoped</u> we would be invited to Caitlin's birthday party.

_____

_____

1

b. Dad <u>snored</u> loudly, so Mum slept in the guest room.

_____

1

Marks

5. Rewrite the sentence below in the **active voice**.

My sister was beaten by Meena in yesterday's cross-country race.

_____

_____

1

6. Underline the **modal verb** in each of the following sentences.

I can count to one hundred in French, but Jake gets stuck after twenty.

Emilie told her teacher she would help her tidy up after the science lesson.

1

7. Write a sentence in the **active voice**.

_____

_____

1

8. Write a sentence in the **passive voice**.

_____

_____

1

9. Complete this sentence with a **modal verb** to show certainty.

I _____ call round with your present later.

Marks

1

10. Write the **present perfect** form of each verb in bold in the sentences below.

Mum **looks** after many people as part of her job as a nurse.

Maia's Dad **takes** the rubbish to the local tip in the boot of his car.

Our cat **drinks** its milk from a saucer.

1

End of test

Marks

SECTION 2: PUNCTUATION

1. Which **punctuation mark** is missing from the place indicated by the arrow?

"What an incredible day that was ͟" sighed Meg as she went upstairs to bed.

Tick **one**.

question mark ☐

comma ☐

full stop ☐

exclamation mark ☐

1

2. Insert **parentheses** in the correct place in each sentence below.

a. We all voted to go on a picnic despite the threat

of rain so everyone helped to make sandwiches

and drinks.

1

b. The weather unusually warm for the time of

year helped make the day extra special.

1

Marks

3. Insert a **colon** in the sentence below.

The views from the mountain top were stunning we

saw lakes, rivers and fields of sheep.

1

4. Rewrite the sentence as **direct speech**, using correct punctuation.

Mrs Courtney said we couldn't go out to play until the classroom had been tidied.

_____

_____

1

5. Explain how the use of **commas** changes the meaning in each sentence below.

Eating too many cakes, which are full of sugar, is bad for your teeth.

Eating too many cakes which are full of sugar is bad for your teeth.

_____

_____

_____

1

6. Write the **contracted form** of each pair or group of words.

Marks

Words	Contracted form	Words	Contracted form
can not		I would	
should have		has not	
she will		Sam is	

1

7. Which sentence uses a **semi-colon** correctly?

Tick **one**.

The bus arrived late yet again; it was the third time this week. ☐

The bus arrived late; yet again it was the third time this week. ☐

The bus arrived late yet again it was the third time; this week. ☐

The bus arrived late yet; again it was the third time this week. ☐

1

Marks

8. Rewrite each sentence below using an **apostrophe** to indicate ownership with the word in bold.

    a. The sword belonging to the prince was found in the woods.

    _____

    _____

1

    b. The swords belonging to the princes were found in the woods.

    _____

    _____

1

9. Insert a **dash** in the sentence below.

It would soon be time to open our presents what would we get this year, we wondered?

1

10. Rewrite the short passage below, correcting the **punctuation** and adding any missing capital letters.

after her fall mrs edward's had to use a wheelchair until her leg was better sadly she could'nt go on holiday to france but her friends daughter said she could stay in her Caravan in devon for a couple of nights

_____

_____

_____

_____ End of test

1

SECTION 2: VOCABULARY

Marks

1. Explain what a **synonym** is.

_____

_____

1

2. Explain what an **antonym** is.

_____

_____

1

3. a. Write a sentence using the word <u>re-cover</u>.

_____

_____

1

b. Write a sentence using the word <u>recover</u>.

_____

_____

1

Marks

4. Which word does not belong to the **word family** below? Write your answer on the line below

benefit   bent   benevolent   beneficial

_____

1

5. Add a **prefix** to each word below to form its **antonym**.

_____material

_____conceivable

_____regard

_____represent

1

6. Change the verbs on the left to adjectives and adverbs by adding suitable **suffixes**.

Verb	Adjective	Adverb
love		
force		
horrify		
rely		

1

7. Insert two **hyphens** in the sentence below to form **compound words** and thus avoid ambiguity.

Mum likes sugar free drinks yet she eats full fat yoghurt.

Marks

1

8. Turn the nouns on the left into adjectives. You may need to change root words before adding suitable **suffixes**.

Noun	Adjective
space	
ambition	
essence	
grace	

1

9. Choose a **homophone** (or **near-homophone**) from the box below to complete the passage.

wandered wondered   whether weather   pouring poring
proceed precede   effect affect   whale wail

We _____ if it was a good idea to go to the beach

as the _____ forecast predicted _____

rain. Dad said we should _____ as planned and

not let a few showers _____ our fun. In the end,

we had a _____ of a time!

1

Marks

10. Which word is similar in meaning to <u>pretend</u>?

Tick **one**.

consider ☐

bluff ☐

demonstrate ☐

reveal ☐

1

11. Each of the verbs below can be changed into a noun and an adjective by adding a suitable **suffix**. You may need to alter the spelling of the root word. Complete the table by writing the new words in the correct column.

| resist | differ | digest | irritate |
| accept | divide | apologise | act |

Noun	Adjective

1

Marks

SECTION 2: STANDARD ENGLISH AND FORMALITY

1. Explain what is meant by **Standard English**.

   _____

   _____

   1

2. Name three things you might find in **formal speech** and **writing**.

   1. _____

   2. _____

   3. _____

   1

3. Name two situations where you would expect **formal speech** and **writing** to be used.

   1. _____

   2. _____

   1

4. Rewrite the sentence below using **Standard English**.

   Me mum said she hadn't got no change for me bus fare.

   _____

   _____

   1

Marks

5. Complete the sentence below using the **subjunctive mood**.

If I _____ to tell you I had royal ancestors, would you believe me?

1

6. Write a short, chatty diary entry using **informal writing**. You can include non-Standard English too.

_____

_____

_____

_____

_____

1

End of test

Marks

SECTION 3: ALL TOPIC AREAS

1. Complete the following sentences using the **present progressive form** of the verbs in brackets.

   a. Since we _____ (move) house this year, we can't afford to go on holiday.

   1

   b. Darius _____ (hope) he will get all his spellings right.

   1

2. Underline the **adverbials** in this sentence.

   The excited crowd applauded wildly as the exhausted runner appeared in the distance.

   1

3. Write a suitable **relative clause** to complete the sentence below.

   Our neighbour Mrs Brown, _____

   _____,

   has received a card from the Queen.

   1

Marks

4. Insert the missing **apostrophes** in the passage below.

Ive been thinking about what to buy for Mums birthday. She needs a new scarf, though in Dads opinion she has loads of scarves. Im pretty sure thats what shell want.

1

5. What is the **function** of the sentence below?

Some people have an aversion to Brussels sprouts.

Tick **one**.

Statement ☐

Command ☐

Exclamation ☐

Question ☐

1

6. Add appropriate **punctuation** to the sentence below.

On our recent holiday to Europe we visited the following tourist attractions the Eiffel Tower in Paris the Princes Palace of Monaco the Leaning Tower of Pisa and the Vatican City in Rome

1

Marks

7. Underline the **subject** and circle the **object** in the sentences below.

    a. My brother Joe usually takes the dog for a walk.

1

    b. Mum's new sewing machine is on the kitchen table.

1

8. Add a **prefix** to each word below to make its **antonym**.

    _____possible

    _____appear

    _____explicable

    _____realistic

1

9. Complete the sentence below so that the verb form uses the **subjunctive mood**.

If you _____ to hear any unfavourable comments about our new range of products, I would be grateful if you could bring them to my attention.

1

Marks

10. Complete the sentence below using the verb <u>try</u> in the **past perfect tense**.

Ushma _____ hard to learn her French vocabulary, but she forgot some words on the day of the test.

1

11. Underline the **adjectives** in the sentence below.

The long-lasting batteries Dad gave me for my new torch barely lasted a week.

1

12. Write a **command** that could be the first step in the instructions for making cheese on toast.

_____

_____

1

Marks

13. Rewrite the sentence below so that it starts with the **adverbial**.

We went for a long walk in the countryside, despite the dreadful rain.

_____

_____

1

14. How does adding the **prefix** <u>dis</u> to the words below change their meaning?

| respect   able   comfort   regard |

Tick **one**.

They become nouns. ☐

They become adverbs. ☐

They become antonyms. ☐

They become synonyms. ☐

1

15. Underline the **subordinate clause** in the sentence below.

Our friends who live in India are coming to see us

at Christmas.

1

16. Tick **one** box in each row to indicate the **word class** of the words in this sentence.

Dad has a new car which he bought last week.

Sentence	Adjective	Adverbial	Verb	Personal pronoun	Determiner	Noun	Relative pronoun
Dad							
has							
a							
new							
car							
which							
he							
bought							
last week							

1

Marks

17. Insert **dashes** to indicate **parenthesis** in the sentence below.

The lion bared its teeth huge, sharp and bloody as it chased its prey.

1

18. Insert suitable **possessive pronouns** in the sentence below.

Those books are _____. I think those are

_____ over there.

1

19. Insert a **relative pronoun** in each sentence below.

a. The lady with _____ my mum goes to yoga has broken her arm.

1

b. The village of Styal, _____ is near Wilmslow, was on the news last night.

1

20. Complete the sentence below by adding a suitable **subordinate clause**.

I'm in trouble with my teacher _____

_____

1

Marks

21. Add a **modal verb** to indicate certainty in the sentence below.

Dad _____ drive us to the cinema later.

1

22. Add a **suffix** to change these adjectives into nouns.

nasty → _____

greedy → _____

weak → _____

1

23. Tick one box in each row to indicate whether the word <u>until</u> is used as a **subordinating conjunction** or as a **preposition**.

Sentence	until used as a subordinating conjunction	until used as a preposition
<u>Until</u> last week, I had been struggling with my homework but now I'm fine.		
We weren't allowed to go outside <u>until</u> we had helped Mum tidy the kitchen.		
Nobody left the room <u>until</u> the teacher dismissed us.		

1

Marks

24. Rewrite the sentence below so that it is in **direct speech**.

The politician said she promised to protect the environment in our local community.

_____

_____

1

25. Underline the **demonstrative determiners** in the sentence below.

Those children have been kicking balls over that fence.

1

26. Write the **plural forms** of the words below.

hutch   _____

woman   _____

patio   _____

kiss   _____

1

Marks

27. Rewrite the **active voice** sentence below in the **passive voice**.

The dedicated author wrote the book in record time.

_____

_____

1

28. Insert the final **punctuation mark** in each of the following sentences.

Can you help me with my homework

I'm not very sure what to do

What a lot of calculations we have to do

Pass me the calculator please

1

29. Rosa said, "**Semi-colons** are only used for marking boundaries between independent clauses."

Is Rosa correct? Circle either **Yes** or **No**.

Yes   No

Explain your reason.

_____

_____

1

Marks

30. Which sentence below uses the **subjunctive mood**?

Tick **one**.

I were really happy when I seen my new bike. ☐

If only I were allowed to ride it to school! ☐

There is a lot of traffic near us which is dangerous. ☐

However, Mum said I'll be able to ride it to Michael's. ☐

1

31. Underline three **common nouns** in the sentence below.

I could see that Zephan's confidence was shattered when

the other team scored but his usual resilience prevailed.

1

32. Tick the sentence that uses a **dash** correctly.

Tick **one**.

Mum's cooking – skills have changed dramatically in the last year definitely for the better. ☐

Mum's cooking skills have changed dramatically in the last year – definitely for the better. ☐

Mum's cooking skills have changed dramatically – in the last year definitely for the better. ☐

Mum's cooking skills have changed – dramatically in the last year definitely for the better. ☐

1

Marks

33. Complete the sentence below with a **verb** formed from the noun speciality.

Mr Hughes _____ in teaching music.

1

34. Rewrite the sentence below so that it starts with the **adverbial**.

We did our homework and tidied our room before bedtime.

_____

_____

1

35. Use only the words in the boxes below to make a sentence.

on their upper jaw

called baleen

have a comb-like fringe

some whales

_____

_____

_____

1

Marks

36. Tick the sentence below that uses **Standard English**.

Tick **one**.

"Have you finished them addition sums yet?" asked Sami. ☐

"I've been working hard on them all morning," sighed Dan. ☐

"You done well in maths last time," said George. ☐

"I seen the answers on the teacher's desk," whispered Kate. ☐

1

37. Change each **noun** on the left by adding a **suffix** to make it a **verb**. Write each verb in the correct column. Change the root word spelling, if necessary.

Noun	Verb
navigation	
solid	
fossil	
strength	

1

38. Underline the longest **expanded noun phrase** in the sentence below.

The old man with the little dog slowly ambled down the winding road.

1

Marks

39. Insert an **apostrophe** to indicate possession in the sentence below.

Our mums cars were parked outside the school.

1

40. Rewrite the sentence below in the **present perfect tense**.

Mum took my younger sister to ballet.

_____

_____

1

41. Circle the **possessive determiners** in the sentence below.

My pet guinea pig has chewed through his cage.

1

42. Tick the sentence that is grammatically correct.

Tick **one**.

Tom and me are taking the bus to the museum this weekend. ☐

The teacher gave Tom and I some information about the exhibitions. ☐

However, Tom had already shown me a website about the museum. ☐

Mum said she would drop him and I at the bus stop. ☐

1

43. Insert a **comma** to show that three items were eaten on the picnic.

Marks

On our picnic, we had vanilla ice-cream cake and strawberry jelly.

1

44. Circle the word below that contains an **apostrophe** for **possession**.

Mr O'Sullivan said he'd give us some of his home-grown carrots and potatoes. He said his wife's rhubarb was also delicious, so we're hoping for a pie.

1

45. Rewrite the sentence below so that it is in the **past perfect tense**.

Our dog gave up hoping for an evening walk.

_____

1

46. Rewrite the sentence below replacing the nouns in bold with a **pronoun**.

The children stood at the top of the mountain and admired the view; **the children** had never seen anything like **the view**.

_____

_____

_____

1

Marks

47. Write the **contracted form** for each group of words below.

did not _____

you have _____

I had _____

was not _____

1

48. Rewrite the sentence below in the **present progressive tense**.

Aisha reads her book in her bedroom.

_____

1

49. Write a **synonym** to replace the word in bold.

The teacher said my homework project was **exceptionally** good.

_____

1

50. Tick the sentence where there is **tense consistency**.

Tick **one**.

Dad drove his car to work but it breaks down before he got there. ☐

It is a tiring day but at long last we had relaxed. ☐

I had been waiting for this moment for years but now my wait was over. ☐

1

51. Why have **brackets** been used in the sentence below?

Marks

My sister's friend (the one she goes dancing with) is performing on stage this weekend.

Tick **one**.

To separate items in a list. ☐

To indicate possession. ☐

To avoid ambiguity. ☐

To indicate a relative clause. ☐

1

52. In the passage below, write the tense of the **verbs in bold** in the box above each. Choose the correct option from the selection you have been given.

| simple past | past perfect | past progressive |

☐

Yesterday, we **started** a new topic in history.

☐

We **were investigating** the causes of World War II.

☐

After Hitler **had invaded** Poland, Britain and France **declared** war on Germany.

☐

1

Marks

53. Jon says, "You can't put an **apostrophe** in 'its' to indicate possession."

Is he correct? Circle **Yes** or **No**.

Yes   No

Explain your answer:

_____

_____

1

54. Add a suitable **prefix** to each word below.

_____acceptable

_____compose

_____biographical

_____definitely

1

55. Rewrite the **active voice** sentences below in the **passive voice**.

Active voice	Passive voice
The brave princess tied the ugly troll to the tree.	
The head teacher warmly welcomed us to the first assembly of the school year.	

1

Marks

56. Complete the sentence below with a suitable **relative pronoun**.

Our neighbour, _____ car had been stolen, reported it to the police.

1

57. Place a tick in the correct row to indicate whether each word in bold is being used as an **adjective** or an **adverb**.

Sentence	Adjective	Adverb
The car drove **fast** around the corner.		
We took the **fast** train to London.		
Nick worked **hard** on his homework.		
It was a **hard** test.		

1

58. Explain how the different **prefixes** change the meaning of the two sentences below.

a. My dad said he had been **unpaid** for his last job.

_____

_____

1

b. My dad said he had been **underpaid** for his last job.

_____

_____

1

Marks

59. **a.** Write a sentence using the word <u>paint</u> as a **verb**.
Do not change the word.

_____

_____

1

b. Now write a sentence using the word <u>paint</u> as a
noun. Do not change the word.

_____

_____

1

End of test

SCHOLASTIC Skills Test Papers

SECTION 3: SPELLING

See Spelling 2 guidance on page 70.
Each correct spelling is worth one mark.

1. We mixed the diluted _____ in the beaker.

2. The rude man did not have the _____ to apologise.

3. We chose our Christmas presents from a

    _____ .

4. My greatest _____ is my Grade 4 piano certificate.

5. The princess was both _____ and kind.

6. We read the first _____ of the play.

7. Our holiday to Spain was a real _____ .

8. I have _____ savings to buy a new tablet.

9. We drew a square-based _____ in maths today.

10. We walked quietly and _____ to the hall.

10

Marks

11. Gran has a collection of antique _____ .

12. Two cars were involved in a _____ outside

    our school.

13. World War II took place in the last _____ .

14. I scratched my ankle on a _____ during

    our walk.

15. Ibrahim likes to _____ the amount

    of pocket money he gets.

16. The doctor _____ Mum to a specialist.

17. School data about pupils is _____ .

18. My sister is _____ as a bit too bossy.

19. Ireland is _____ my favourite

    holiday destination.

20. We had an _____ Christmas tree

    this year.

10

End of test

GUIDANCE FOR SECTION 1: SPELLING

SPELLING TEST INSTRUCTIONS

1. For each word say: "The word is _____."

2. Read the example sentence.

3. Then repeat: "The word is _____."

Q	Word	Example sentence
1	irritable	My brother can be very **irritable** in the mornings.
2	closure	The villagers were very annoyed about the **closure** of the church hall.
3	bought	Sinead **bought** her mum a bunch of flowers.
4	clearance	The pilot was given **clearance** to land.
5	science	We have two **science** lessons per week.
6	confidence	Stella displayed great **confidence** as she prepared to dive.
7	machine	My mum uses a sewing **machine** to make curtains.
8	occupy	We took games to **occupy** ourselves on the long flight.
9	noticeable	The scar on my finger is now hardly **noticeable**.
10	dynamic	Dad's new boss is **dynamic**, extrovert and fun-loving.
11	regularly	Juan **regularly** goes to Spain in the holidays.
12	vague	Mum gave Dad **vague** instructions about preparing the meal.
13	unquestionably	Summer term is **unquestionably** the best.
14	gullible	My **gullible** best friend believes everything I tell him!
15	halved	Billy and I **halved** the last piece of cake.
16	desperate	The children were **desperate** to get to the seaside.
17	politician	The **politician** made a speech about his party's policy.
18	reign	The Queen has had the longest **reign** of any British monarch.
19	weight	I staggered under the **weight** of the heavy box.
20	disciplined	Our teacher **disciplined** us for talking in assembly.

GUIDANCE FOR SECTION 3: SPELLING

SPELLING TEST INSTRUCTIONS

1. For each word say: "The word is _____."

2. Read the example sentence.

3. Then repeat: "The word is _____."

Q	Word	Example sentence
1	substance	We mixed the diluted **substance** in the beaker.
2	decency	The rude man did not have the **decency** to apologise.
3	catalogue	We chose our Christmas presents from a **catalogue**.
4	achievement	My greatest **achievement** is my Grade 4 piano certificate.
5	gracious	The princess was both **gracious** and kind.
6	scene	We read the first **scene** of the play.
7	bargain	Our holiday to Spain was a real **bargain**.
8	sufficient	I have **sufficient** savings to buy a new tablet.
9	pyramid	We drew a square-based **pyramid** in maths today.
10	sensibly	We walked quietly and **sensibly** to the hall.
11	jewellery	Gran has a collection of antique **jewellery**.
12	collision	Two cars were involved in a **collision** outside our school.
13	century	World War II took place in the last **century**.
14	thistle	I scratched my ankle on a **thistle** during our walk.
15	exaggerate	Ibrahim likes to **exaggerate** the amount of pocket money he gets.
16	referred	The doctor **referred** Mum to a specialist.
17	confidential	School data about pupils is **confidential**.
18	perceived	My sister is **perceived** as a bit too bossy.
19	undoubtedly	Ireland is **undoubtedly** my favourite holiday destination.
20	artificial	We had an **artificial** Christmas tree this year.

Answers

The answers are given below. They are referenced by page number and question number. The answers usually only include the information the children are expected to give. There may be some places where the answers vary or multiple answers are acceptable, these are marked as such.

Note that in some places, answers will be varied and subjective from child to child, and a fair degree of marker discretion and interpretation is needed, particularly if children's understanding and skills have to be deduced from their answers.

Question	Answers	Marks
Section 1: All topic areas (pages 8–26)		
1	As the <u>galloping</u> horses cleared the <u>final</u> fence, the crowd applauded wildly.	1
2	a. Just as we **were approaching** our destination, the traffic became more and more congested. b. My sister Megan **was arranging** flowers in a vase for Mum.	1 1
3	It's been five years since I've seen my cousins, Stephane and Anya. Stephane's dress-sense was always slightly unusual and Anya's smile was infectious. Mum's very excited about seeing her sister again and she's promised we'll all go out for a meal as soon as they've unpacked.	2
4	Command	1
5	Accept an appropriate relative clause, for example: Our teacher Mr Harrison, **who has taught at the school for a long time**, is retiring next year.	1
6	a. <u>Ciara's mum</u> was pleased with (her presents.) b. <u>Some careless person</u> has left (the door) open.	1 1
7	**im**practical / **un**decided / **in**accessible / **il**legitimate	1
8	Accept a suitable verb in the present perfect tense, for example: We **have lived** in the same house for ten years.	1
9	At the circus, we saw the following**:** trapeze artists**;** performing ponies**;** a high-wire act and a rather sad clown**.** (Also accept commas instead of semi-colons and a dash instead of the colon.)	1
10	Accept an appropriate question, correctly punctuated. For example: What will the weather be like tomorrow?	1
11	Accept an appropriate fronted adverbial followed by a comma. For example: **After a long climb,** we eventually reached the summit. Or: **At long last,** we eventually reached the summit.	1
12	They mean the opposite.	1
13	If I **were** to approach the manager in the correct way, I am positive he would respond favourably to my request.	1
14	After we had eaten our breakfast, we <u>quickly</u> tidied up and went <u>outside.</u>	1
15	Our former neighbours**,** John and Josephine**,** came to visit us today.	1

Answers

Question	Answers	Marks
	Section 1: All topic areas (pages 8–26) continued	
16	a. The little boy, **whose** parents were late to pick him up, was very upset. b. Our grandparents, with **whom** we stay every summer, are coming to visit us this year.	1 1
17	Dad likes to listen to music on his headphones **as/when/while** he cuts the grass.	1

Sentence	Adjective	Adverb	Verb	Pronoun	Possessive determiner	Noun	Conjunction
Our					✓		
old	✓						
dog						✓	
always		✓					
shivers			✓				
when							✓
he				✓			
is			✓				
cold	✓						

(Question 18 — 1 mark)

Question	Answers	Marks
19	petti**ness** / empti**ness** / full**ness**	1
20	We **may/might/could/should** go to Spain for our holidays this year.	1
21	Those cakes are <u>mine</u>; I made them in school today. Khalid made some too but <u>his</u> are slightly burnt.	1
22	"We need to pack our clothes tonight," said Mum. "Can't I wait until the morning**?**" I asked**.** "It will be too rushed if you leave it until the morning**,**" she replied**.**	1
23	**ir**regular / **dis**continue / **un**reliable / **im**probable	1
24	<u>Some</u> people eat <u>their</u> lunch on <u>the</u> field on sunny days, but I prefer to stay in <u>the</u> shade.	1
25	Millie is not correct. Accept an answer that makes reference to one of the following: a pair of commas can be used to indicate parenthesis; after a fronted adverbial or fronted clause; at the end of direct speech before the final inverted commas; for clarity; after a co-ordinating conjunction linking two independent clauses.	1
26	Liam crept cautiously towards the entrance to the cave – surely the creature was no longer there?	1

Sentence	**after** used as a subordinating conjunction	**after** used as a preposition
<u>After</u> I had finished my homework, I watched a film with Dad.	✓	
The animals in the zoo like to snooze <u>after</u> they've eaten.	✓	
I'm going to Ushma's house <u>after</u> school.		✓

(Question 27 — 1 mark)

Question	Answers	Marks
	Section 1: All topic areas (pages 8–26) continued	
28	The aerial on our roof needs to be fixed	1
29	While we were away, our pet tortoise was looked after by our neighbour. Or: Our pet tortoise was looked after by our neighbour while we were away.	1
30	How excited I was	1
31	After their long hike up the mountain, Luke and Heba were exhausted.	1
32	Accept any one of the following: My friend Bethan, who has just moved house, is coming to stay this weekend. This weekend, my friend Bethan, who has just moved house, is coming to stay. My friend Bethan who has just moved house is coming to stay this weekend. This weekend, my friend Bethan who has just moved house is coming to stay.	1
33	After <u>a long, hard day</u>, Jo was glad to get home and relax on the settee.	1
34	There's no point in worrying about the test.	1
35	I **have eaten** some interesting dishes during my holiday.	1
36	prioritise / signify / indicate	1
37	Our teacher handed Freya and **me** our books. Freya and **I** were thrilled with our results.	1
38	church**es** / child**ren** / piano**s** / class**es**	1
39	What a wonderful day that was**!** Do you think we can do it again soon**?** The weather forecast looks promising for tomorrow**.** What time do you think we should meet**?**	1
40	We have decided**,** since the snow seems to be sticking**,** that we will go sledging in the park.	1
41	sigh	1
42	<u>Their</u> grandparents are thinking of moving closer to <u>our</u> neighbourhood so that they can see more of <u>their</u> grandchildren.	1
43	We had finished our jobs so we were free to play.	1
44	<table><tr><th>Genre</th><th>Formal</th><th>Informal</th></tr><tr><td>Diary writing</td><td></td><td>✓</td></tr><tr><td>Presentation in a job interview</td><td>✓</td><td></td></tr><tr><td>Postcard</td><td></td><td>✓</td></tr><tr><td>Persuasive letter to the local council</td><td>✓</td><td></td></tr></table>	1
45	haven't / you'll / she's / shan't	1
46	Mel **is jumping** on the trampoline.	1
47	There are the boys **whose** bikes were stolen yesterday.	1
48	Bethan and Freddy are good friends; **they** have known each other for years.	1
49	Answers will vary. Accept appropriate expanded noun phrases, for example: **The beautiful butterfly** fluttered over **the colourful flowers** and landed on **a prickly bush.**	1
50	Next week, Leila **will** take her Grade 3 piano exam.	1
51	Answers will vary. Accept a suitable synonym for <u>unbelievably</u>, for example: incredibly.	1

Answers

Question	Answers	Marks
	Section 1: All topic areas (pages 8–26) continued	
52	After we **had been** to the zoo, we went for something to eat.	1
53	<table><tr><th>Passive voice</th><th>Active voice</th></tr><tr><td>Our car was washed by an expert cleaning crew.</td><td>An expert cleaning crew washed our car.</td></tr><tr><td>After I twisted my ankle, I was helped up the stairs by my friend Anna.</td><td>My friend Anna helped me up the stairs after I twisted my ankle. Or: After I twisted my ankle, my friend Anna helped me up the stairs.</td></tr></table>	1
54	To indicate parenthesis.	1
55	As they neared the end of the marathon, the runners began to fantasise about a cold drink and a hot bath. (The fronted clause must be followed by a comma for the award of 1 mark.)	1
56	a. The naughty girl picked off the flower's petals one by one. Explanation: 'flower' is singular in this sentence.	1
	b. The naughty girl picked off the flowers' petals one by one. Explanation: 'flower' is plural in this sentence.	1
57	The bird suddenly swooped down towards (its nest.)	1
58	**auto**matic / **in**human or **un**human / **sub**human / **mis**fortune / **pre**view or **over**view or **re**view	1
59	Sam worked hard on her school project but it was worth it.	1
60	The girl showed a lot of courage when faced with the ugly creature.	1
61	We **were walking [past progressive]** towards the park when we **saw [simple past]** a fire engine flying down the road. We **had seen [past perfect]** an ambulance go past only ten minutes before. Hopefully, no one **had been [past perfect]** badly hurt.	1
62	The mouse chased the cat around the garden.	1
	Section 2: Word classes (pages 29–30)	
1	Answers will vary. For example: a. hike as a noun: We thoroughly enjoyed our **hike** up the mountain.	1
	b. hike as a verb: Mum and Dad like to **hike** as a pastime.	1
2	Finally (D), we reached (A) the island (B) which was surrounded by crashing (C) waves.	1
3	We gave Mia a present and she was pleased with it.	1
4	Our teacher was very **understanding** when we handed our homework in late.	1
5	<table><tr><th>Noun</th><th>Adjective</th></tr><tr><td>care</td><td>care**ful**/care**less**</td></tr><tr><td>noise</td><td>nois**y**/noise**less**</td></tr><tr><td>pity</td><td>piti**ful**/piti**less**</td></tr><tr><td>beauty</td><td>beauti**ful**</td></tr></table>	1
6	**Those** / **these** dogs are barking at **that** / **this** postman.	1
7	Archie passed the butter to **his** sister so she could butter **her** toast.	1
8	Fast is used as an adjective because it is describing the train.	1

SCHOLASTIC Skills Test Papers

Question	Answers	Marks
Section 2: Functions of sentences (pages 31–32)		
1	My mum makes a great Sunday roast dinner	1
2	That girl is from our town.	1
3	Answers may vary. Accept any appropriate question, correctly punctuated. For example: Do you have any pets?	1
4	Answers will vary. For example: Please **finish** your homework before the weekend.	1
5	The bus is late today, isn't it?	1
6	How many days until Christmas — statement How excited I am about Christmas — question There are thirteen days until Christmas — command Tell me how many days there are until Christmas — exclamation	1
Section 2: Combining words, phrases and clauses (pages 33–34)		

	Sentence	Subordinating conjunction	Co-ordinating conjunction
1	We have been playing rounders and tennis this term.		✓
	Before I leave for school, I always make my packed lunch.	✓	
	It's been quite cold, yet it's not quite the end of summer.		✓
	I saw your cousin in the library, but I couldn't remember her name.		✓

Marks: 1

Question	Answers	Marks
2	Our teacher said we would stay in at break **unless** we behaved.	1
3	relative clause	1
4	With only minutes to go, <u>the exhausted runners</u> pushed themselves towards the finish.	1
5	main clause	1
6	Answers will vary. For example: My new school, **which I started in September**, has lots of extra-curricular activities. Or: My new school, **which is called Newbank Primary**, has lots of extra-curricular activities.	1
Section 2: Verb forms, tense and consistency (pages 35–38)		
1	We were thinking of going to the cinema but now we've changed our minds.	1
2	I was given a choice of salad or vegetables.	1

Verb	Simple present	Simple past	Present progressive	Past progressive	Present perfect	Past perfect
they were thinking				✓		
we have seen					✓	
Pippa plays	✓					
you had written						✓
George is eating			✓			
she spoke		✓				

Marks (question 3): 1

Answers

Question	Answers	Marks
\multicolumn{3}{l}{**Section 2: Verb forms, tense and consistency (pages 35–38) continued**}		
4	a. We **were hoping** we would be invited to Caitlin's birthday party. b. Dad **was snoring** loudly, so Mum slept in the guest room.	1 1
5	Meena beat my sister in yesterday's cross-country race.	1
6	I <u>can</u> count to one hundred in French, but Jake gets stuck after twenty. Emilie told her teacher she <u>would</u> help her tidy up after the science lesson.	1
7	Any suitable sentence, correctly punctuated, in the active voice.	1
8	Any suitable sentence, correctly punctuated, in the passive voice.	1
9	I **will/shall** call round with your present later.	1
10	Mum **has looked** after many people as part of her job as a nurse. Maia's Dad **has taken** the rubbish to the local tip in the boot of his car. Our cat **has drunk** its milk from a saucer.	1

Section 2: Punctuation (pages 39–42)

Question	Answers	Marks
1	exclamation mark	1
2	Accept a pair of dashes, commas or brackets. For example: a. We all voted to go on a picnic – despite the threat of rain – so everyone helped to make sandwiches and drinks. b. The weather (unusually warm for the time of year) helped make the day extra special.	1 1
3	The views from the mountain top were stunning: we saw lakes, rivers and fields of sheep.	1
4	Mrs Courtney said, "You can't go out to play until the classroom has been tidied." Or: "You can't go out to play until the classroom has been tidied," said Mrs Courtney.	1
5	Accept answers that refer to the following differences: The first sentence implies that all cakes are full of sugar. The second sentence implies that if you eat only those cakes that are full of sugar, it is bad for your teeth.	1
6	<table><tr><th>Words</th><th>Contracted form</th><th>Words</th><th>Contracted form</th></tr><tr><td>can not</td><td>can't</td><td>I would</td><td>I'd</td></tr><tr><td>should have</td><td>should've</td><td>has not</td><td>hasn't</td></tr><tr><td>she will</td><td>she'll</td><td>Sam is</td><td>Sam's</td></tr></table>	1
7	The bus arrived late yet again; it was the third time this week.	1
8	a. The prince's sword was found in the woods. b. The princes' swords were found in the woods.	1 1
9	It would soon be time to open our presents – what would we get this year, we wondered?	1
10	**A**fter her fall**,** **M**rs **E**dward**s** had to use a wheelchair until her leg was better**.** **S**adly**,** she could**n't** go on holiday to **F**rance but her friend's daughter said she could stay in her **c**aravan in **D**evon for a couple of nights**.** (Also accept <u>friends'</u>.)	1

Section 2: Vocabulary (pages 43–46)

Question	Answers	Marks
1	A synonym is a word that means the same or almost the same as another word.	1
2	An antonym is a word that has the opposite meaning of another word.	1

SCHOLASTIC Skills Test Papers

Question	Answers	Marks
Section 2: Vocabulary (pages 43–46) continued		
3	Answers will vary. For example: a. Mum decided to **re-cover** our old settee. b. After a long illness, Gran slowly began to **recover**.	1 1
4	bent	1
5	**im**material / **in**conceivable / **dis**regard / **mis**represent	1

	Verb	Adjective	Adverb
6	love	lovely / loveable	loveably / lovingly
	force	forceful / forcible	forcibly / forcefully
	horrify	horrible / horrific	horribly / horrifically
	rely	reliable	reliably

(Marks: 1)

Question	Answers	Marks
7	Mum likes sugar**-**free drinks yet she eats full**-**fat yoghurt.	1

	Noun	Adjective
8	space	spacious
	ambition	ambitious
	essence	essential
	grace	gracious/graceful

(Marks: 1)

Question	Answers	Marks
9	We **wondered** if it was a good idea to go to the beach as the **weather** forecast predicted **pouring** rain. Dad said we should **proceed** as planned and not let a few showers **affect** our fun. In the end, we had a **whale** of a time!	1
10	bluff	1

	Noun	Adjective
11	resistance	resistible
	difference	different
	digestion	digestible
	irritation	irritable / irritating
	acceptance	acceptable
	division	divisible / divisive
	apology	apologetic
	action	active

(Marks: 1)

Question	Answers	Marks
Section 2: Standard English and formality (pages 47–48)		
1	Standard English is using grammatically correct speech and writing. It can be formal or informal.	1
2	Any three from: formal vocabulary, passive voice, subjunctive mood, Standard English.	1
3	Answers will vary. For example: a letter to your head teacher, an interview, an introduction of a guest speaker, school report.	1
4	My mum said she hadn't got any change for my bus fare.	1

Answers

Question	Answers	Marks
	**Section 2: Standard English and formality (pages 47–48) continued**	
5	If I **were** to tell you I had royal ancestors, would you believe me?	1
6	Answers will vary. Should be informal and chatty and can contain slang, abbreviations and colloquialisms.	1
	**Section 3: All topic areas (pages 49–68)**	
1	a. Since we **are moving** house this year, we can't afford to go on holiday. b. Darius **is hoping** he will get all his spellings right.	1 1
2	The excited crowd applauded <u>wildly</u> as the exhausted runner appeared <u>in the distance</u>.	1
3	Answers will vary. For example: Our neighbour Mrs Brown, **who does a lot of work for charity**, has received a card from the Queen.	1
4	I've been thinking about what to buy for Mum's birthday. She needs a new scarf, though in Dad's opinion she has loads of scarves. I'm pretty sure that's what she'll want.	1
5	Statement	1
6	On our recent holiday to Europe, we visited the following tourist attractions: the Eiffel Tower in Paris; the Prince's Palace of Monaco; the Leaning Tower of Pisa; and the Vatican City in Rome. (Also accept commas between the listed attractions.)	1
7	a. <u>My brother Joe</u> usually takes (the dog) for a walk. b. <u>Mum's new sewing machine</u> is on (the kitchen table.)	1 1
8	**im**possible / **dis**appear / **in**explicable / **un**realistic	1
9	If you **were** to hear any unfavourable comments about our new range of products, I would be grateful if you could bring them to my attention.	1
10	Ushma **had tried** hard to learn her French vocabulary but she forgot some words on the day of the test.	1
11	The <u>long-lasting</u> batteries Dad gave me for my <u>new</u> torch barely lasted a week.	1
12	Answers will vary. For example: First, grate some cheese.	1
13	Despite the dreadful rain, we went for a long walk in the countryside.	1
14	They become antonyms.	1
15	Our friends <u>who live in India</u> are coming to see us at Christmas.	1

Question	Sentence	Adjective	Adverbial	Verb	Personal pronoun	Determiner	Noun	Relative pronoun	Marks
16	Dad						✓		1
	has			✓					
	a					✓			
	new	✓							
	car						✓		
	which							✓	
	he				✓				
	bought			✓					
	last week		✓						

Question	Answers	Marks
17	The lion bared its teeth – huge, sharp and bloody – as it chased its prey.	1

Question	Answers	Marks
	Section 3: All topic areas (pages 49–68) continued	
18	Those books are **mine/yours/his/hers/ours/theirs.** I think those are **mine/yours/his/hers/ours/theirs** over there.	1
19	a. The lady with **whom** my mum goes to yoga has broken her arm. b. The village of Styal, **which** is near Wilmslow, was on the news last night.	1 1
20	Answers will vary. For example: I'm in trouble with my teacher **because I didn't do my homework.**	1
21	Dad **will** drive us to the cinema later.	1
22	nast**iness** / greed**iness** / weak**ness**	1

23	Sentence	until used as a subordinating conjunction	until used as a preposition	Marks
	Until last week, I had been struggling with my homework but now I'm fine.		✓	
	We weren't allowed to go outside until we had helped Mum tidy the kitchen.	✓		1
	Nobody left the room until the teacher dismissed us.	✓		

Question	Answers	Marks
24	The politician said, "I promise to protect the environment in our local community." Or: "I promise to protect the environment in our local community," said the politician.	1
25	<u>Those</u> children have been kicking balls over <u>that</u> fence.	1
26	hutches / women / patios / kisses	1
27	The book was written by the dedicated author in record time. Or: The book was written in record time by the dedicated author.	1
28	Can you help me with my homework**?** I'm not very sure what to do**.** What a lot of calculations we have to do**!** Pass me the calculator please**.** (Also accept an exclamation mark here.)	1
29	Rosa is not correct because semi-colons can also separate longer items in a list.	1
30	If only I were allowed to ride it to school!	1
31	I could see that Zephan's <u>confidence</u> was shattered when the other <u>team</u> scored but his usual <u>resilience</u> prevailed.	1
32	Mum's cooking skills have changed dramatically in the last year – definitely for the better.	1
33	Mr Hughes **specialises** in teaching music.	1
34	Before bedtime, we did our homework and tidied our room.	1
35	Some whales have a comb-like fringe called baleen on their upper jaw. Or: Some whales have a comb-like fringe on their upper jaw called baleen.	1
36	"I've been working hard on them all morning," sighed Dan.	1

Answers

Question	Answers	Marks
	Section 3: All topic areas (pages 49–68) continued	

	Noun	Verb	
37	navigation	navigate / navigates	1
	solid	solidify / solidifies	
	fossil	fossilise / fossilises	
	strength	strengthen / strengthens	

Question	Answers	Marks
38	<u>The old man with the little dog</u> slowly ambled down the winding road.	1
39	Our mums' cars were parked outside the school.	1
40	Mum **has taken** my younger sister to ballet.	1
41	(My) pet guinea pig has chewed through (his) cage.	1
42	However, Tom had already shown me a website about the museum.	1
43	On our picnic, we had vanilla ice-cream**,** cake and strawberry jelly.	1
44	Mr O'Sullivan said he'd give us some of his home-grown carrots and potatoes. He said his wife's rhubarb was also delicious, so we're hoping for a pie.	1
45	Our dog **had given up** hoping for an evening walk.	1
46	The children stood at the top of the mountain and admired the view; **they** had never seen anything like **it**.	1
47	didn't / you've/ I'd / wasn't	1
48	Aisha **is reading** her book in her bedroom.	1
49	Answers will vary. For example: particularly	1
50	I had been waiting for this moment for years but now my wait was over.	1
51	To avoid ambiguity.	1
52	Yesterday, we **started [simple past]** a new topic in history. We **were investigating [past progressive]** the causes of World War II. After Hitler **had invaded [past perfect]** Poland, Britain and France **declared [simple past]** war on Germany.	1
53	Jon is correct because **it's** can only mean *it is* or *it has*.	1
54	**un**acceptable / **de**compose / **auto**biographical / **in**definitely	1

	Active voice	Passive voice	
55	The brave princess tied the ugly troll to the tree.	The ugly troll was tied to the tree by the brave princess.	1
	The head teacher warmly welcomed us to the first assembly of the school year.	We were warmly welcomed to the first assembly of the school year by the head teacher.	

Question	Answers	Marks
56	Our neighbour, **whose** car had been stolen, reported it to the police.	1

	Sentence	Adjective	Adverb	
57	The car drove **fast** around the corner.		✓	1
	We took the **fast** train to London.	✓		
	Nick worked **hard** on his homework.		✓	
	It was a **hard** test.	✓		

Question	Answers	Marks
	Section 3: All topic areas (pages 49–68) continued	
58	a. My dad said he had been **unpaid** for his last job. (Means my dad had not been paid at all.)	1
	b. My dad said he had been **underpaid** for his last job. (Means my dad had not been paid enough.)	1
59	Answers will vary. For example:	
	a. Rob said he would **paint** the picture using acrylics.	1
	b. Rob spilled the **paint** all over the table.	1

Answer grids

Answer grids

Section 1: All topic areas

Q	Topic	Possible marks	Actual marks	Workbook links
1	Word classes	1		6–7
2	Verb forms, tense and consistency	2		20–23
3	Punctuation	2		32–35
4	Functions of sentences	1		12–13
5	Verb forms, tense and consistency	1		16–17
6	Word classes	1		24–25
7	Vocabulary	1		38–39
8	Verb forms, tense and consistency	1		20–23
9	Punctuation	1		28–29
10	Functions of sentences	1		12–13
11	Word classes	1		6–7
12	Vocabulary	1		38–39
13	Verb forms, tense and consistency Standard English and formality	1		44–45
14	Word classes	1		6–7, 10–11
15	Punctuation	1		26–27
16	Word classes	2		16–17
17	Combining words, phrases and clauses	1		14–15
18	Word classes	1		6–7
19	Vocabulary	1		40–41
20	Verb forms, tense and consistency	1		10–11
21	Word classes	1		8–9
22	Punctuation	1		36–37
23	Vocabulary	1		38–39, 42–43
24	Word classes	1		8–9
25	Punctuation	1		26–27, 30–31
26	Punctuation	1		26–27, 28–29
27	Combining words, phrases and clauses Word classes	1		14–15

Section 1: All topic areas continued

Q	Topic	Possible marks	Actual marks	Workbook links
28	Functions of sentences	1		12–13
29	Verb forms, tense and consistency	1		24–25
30	Functions of sentences	1		12–13
31	Word classes	1		6–7
32	Combining words, phrases and clauses	1		14–15
33	Combining words, phrases and clauses	1		18–19
34	Standard English and formality	1		44–45
35	Verb forms, tense and consistency	1		20–23
36	Vocabulary	1		40–41
37	Word classes	1		8–9
38	Vocabulary	1		40–41
39	Punctuation	1		12–13
40	Punctuation	1		30–31
41	Vocabulary	1		38–39, 48–49
42	Word classes	1		8–9
43	Verb forms, tense and consistency	1		20–23
44	Standard English and formality	1		44–45
45	Punctuation	1		32–33
46	Verb forms, tense and consistency	1		20–23
47	Word classes	1		16–17
48	Word classes	1		8–9
49	Combining words, phrases and clauses	1		18–19
50	Verb forms, tense and consistency	1		10–11
51	Vocabulary	1		42–43
52	Verb forms, tense and consistency	1		20–23
53	Verb forms, tense and consistency	1		24–25
54	Punctuation	1		26–27
55	Combining words, phrases and clauses	1		14–15
56	Punctuation	2		34–35
57	Word classes	1		24–25
58	Vocabulary	1		38–39
59	Word classes	1		10–11
60	Word classes	1		6–7
61	Verb forms, tense and consistency	1		20–23
62	Word classes	1		24–25

Answer grids

Section 2

Tests	Possible marks	Actual marks
Word classes	9	
Functions of sentences	6	
Combining words, phrases and clauses	6	
Verb forms, tense and consistency	11	
Punctuation	12	
Vocabulary	12	
Standard English and formality	6	

Section 3: All topic areas

Q	Topic	Possible marks	Actual marks	Workbook links
1	Verb forms, tense and consistency	2		20–23
2	Word classes	1		6–7
3	Combining words, phrases and clauses	1		16–17
4	Punctuation	1		32–35
5	Functions of sentences	1		12–13
6	Punctuation	1		28–29
7	Word classes	2		24–25
8	Vocabulary	1		38–39, 42–43
9	Verb forms, tense and consistency Standard English and formality	1		44–45
10	Verb forms, tense and consistency	1		20–23
11	Word classes	1		6–7
12	Functions of sentences	1		12–13
13	Word classes	1		6–7
14	Vocabulary	1		38–39
15	Combining words, phrases and clauses	1		14–15
16	Word classes	1		6–7
17	Punctuation	1		26–27
18	Word classes	1		8–9
19	Word classes	2		16–17
20	Combining words, phrases and clauses	1		14–15

SCHOLASTIC Skills Test Papers

Answer grids

Section 3: All topic areas continued

Q	Topic	Possible marks	Actual marks	Workbook links
21	Verb forms, tense and consistency	1		10–11
22	Vocabulary	1		40–41
23	Word classes Combining words, phrases and clauses	1		14–15
24	Punctuation	1		36–37
25	Word classes	1		8–9
26	Vocabulary	1		40–41
27	Verb forms, tense and consistency	1		24–25
28	Punctuation	1		12–13
29	Punctuation	1		28–29
30	Verb forms, tense and consistency Standard English and formality	1		44–45
31	Word classes	1		6–7
32	Punctuation	1		26–27, 28–29
33	Verb forms, tense and consistency	1		40–41
34	Word classes	1		6–7
35	Combining words, phrases and clauses	1		14–15
36	Standard English and formality	1		44–45
37	Word classes Vocabulary	1		40–41
38	Combining words, phrases and clauses	1		18–19
39	Punctuation	1		34–35
40	Verb forms, tense and consistency	1		20–23
41	Word classes	1		8–9
42	Verb forms, tense and consistency	1		20–23, 44–45
43	Punctuation	1		30–31
44	Punctuation	1		34–35
45	Verb forms, tense and consistency	1		20–23
46	Word classes	1		8–9
47	Punctuation	1		32–33
48	Verb forms, tense and consistency	1		20–23
49	Vocabulary	1		42–43

Answer grids

Section 3: All topic areas continued

Q	Topic	Possible marks	Actual marks	Workbook links
50	Verb forms, tense and consistency	1		20–23
51	Punctuation	1		26–27
52	Verb forms, tense and consistency	1		20–23
53	Punctuation	1		32–35
54	Vocabulary	1		38–39
55	Verb forms, tense and consistency	1		24–25
56	Word classes	1		16–17
57	Word classes	1		6–7
58	Vocabulary	2		38–39
59	Word classes	2		6–7

SCHOLASTIC Skills Test Papers